Ireland

by Janice Clark Rudolph

Consultant: Marjorie Faulstich Orellana, PhD
Professor of Urban Schooling
University of California, Los Angeles

BEARPORT
PUBLISHING

New York, New York

Credits

Cover, © kalmatsuy/Shutterstock; TOC, © ULKASTUDIO/Shutterstock; 4, © Gareth McCormack/Alamy Stock Photo; 5T, © IG_Royal/iStock; 5B, © matthi/Shutterstock; 7, © VanderWolf Images/Shutterstock; 8TL, © kanawat/Shutterstock; 8BL, © stephenkiernan/Shutterstock and CHAIWATPHOTOS/Shutterstock; 8–9, © Federica Violin/Shutterstock; 10, © Private Collection/The Stapleton Collection/Bridgeman Images; 11T, © Georgios Kollidas/Shutterstock; 11B, © DejaVuDesigns/Shutterstock; 12T, Public Domain; 12B, © Tony Cunningham/Alamy Stock Photo; 13, © Sue Heaton/Alamy Stock Photo; 14, © Illustrated London News Ltd/Mary Evans/AGE Fotostock; 15, © Design Pics Inc/Alamy Stock Photo; 16–17, © Bart_Kowski/iStock; 17L, © drew farrell/Alamy Stock Photo; 18, © Look and Learn/Bridgeman Images; 19, © Peter Oshkai/Alamy Stock Photo; 20, © Editorial12/iStock; 21, © JoeFoxBerlin/Radharc Images/Alamy Stock Photo; 22T, © Fabiano's_Photo/Shutterstock; 22B, © Newscast Online Limited/Alamy Stock Photo; 23T, © NiKreative/Alamy Stock Photo; 24, © Brent Hofacker/Shutterstock; 25T, © AS Food studio/Shutterstock; 25B, © Martin Siepmann/imageBROKER/Alamy Stock Photo; 26L, © Grigorita Ko/Shutterstock; 26R, © Rosa Jay/Shutterstock; 27, © A. Tamboly/Westend61 GmbH/Alamy Stock Photo; 28, © Barry Cronin/Alamy Stock Photo; 29T, © JoeFoxBelfast/Radharc Images/Alamy Stock Photo; 29B, © Neil Paterson/Alamy Stock Photo; 30T, © Tony Kunz/Shutterstock and © spinetta/Shutterstock; 30B, © John Benson/CC BY 4.0; 31 (T to B), © anetapics/Shutterstock, © Bart_Kowski/iStock, Public Domain, © Wavebreakmedia/Shutterstock, and Public Domain; 32, © tristan tan/Shutterstock.

Publisher: Kenn Goin
Editor: J. Clark
Creative Director: Spencer Brinker
Design: Debrah Kaiser
Photo Researcher: Thomas Persano

Library of Congress Cataloging-in-Publication Data

Names: Rudolph, Janice Clark, author.
Title: Ireland / by Janice Clark Rudolph.
Description: New York, New York : Bearport Publishing, 2018. | Series:
   Countries we come from | Includes bibliographical references and index.
Identifiers: LCCN 2017007440 (print) | LCCN 2017011315 (ebook) | ISBN
   9781684022540 (library bound) | ISBN 9781684023080 (ebook)
Subjects: LCSH: Ireland—Juvenile literature.
Classification: LCC DA906 .R83 2018 (print) | LCC DA906 (ebook) | DDC
   941.7—dc23
LC record available at https://lccn.loc.gov/2017007440

For more information, write to Bearport Publishing Company, Inc., 45 West 21st Street, Suite 3B, New York, New York 10010. Printed in the United States of America.

10 9 8 7 6 5 4 3 2 1

Contents

Green

Welcoming

Historic

Ireland is a country in Europe.

It shares an island with the country of Northern Ireland.

Northern
Ireland
(UK)

Ireland

Arctic Ocean

NORTH
AMERICA

EUROPE

ASIA

Atlantic
Ocean

AFRICA

Pacific
Ocean

Pacific
Ocean

SOUTH
AMERICA

Indian
Ocean

AUSTRALIA

N

W   E

S

Southern Ocean

ANTARCTICA

Almost five million people live in Ireland.

Ireland is known as the Emerald Isle because it's so green.

The center of the country has rolling green hills.

an emerald

The longest river in Ireland is the River Shannon. It's 224 miles (360 km) long.

Steep cliffs curve along the shores.

the Cliffs of Moher

There are hundreds of small islands off Ireland's coasts.

Different groups have controlled Ireland over the years.

The Vikings invaded in the 700s.

They built cities, such as Dublin.

Then the English took control almost 1,000 years ago.

They ruled the Irish people unfairly for many centuries.

Henry II, an English king who ruled in the 1100s

Celtic people arrived in Ireland around 500 BC. They left ruins of forts and other buildings.

In the mid-1800s, the Irish people faced the Great **Famine**.

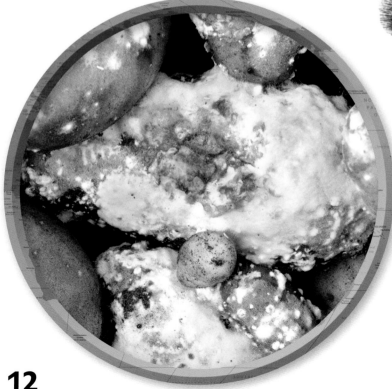

A disease called blight damaged the potato crop in Ireland.

Potatoes were a big part of the Irish diet, so there was very little to eat.

From 1845 to 1849, about one million people died of starvation or disease.

For hundreds of years, the Irish fought for their freedom from England.

One famous **uprising**, the Easter Rising, occurred in 1916.

Many people died.

Finally, in 1922, the Irish Free State was formed.

The Irish people had their own country, but it was still a part of the United Kingdom.

In 1949, Ireland became a completely independent country.

The **capital** of Ireland is Dublin.

It's also the largest city in the country.

About one million people live there.

Many famous people, such as Bono, are from Dublin. Bono is the lead singer of the rock group U2.

March 17 is a big day in Ireland.

It's Saint Patrick's Day.

Saint Patrick spread Christianity throughout Ireland in the 400s.

Legend says that Saint Patrick drove all the snakes out of Ireland!

People honor him with parades.

In Ireland, most people speak English.

However, children also learn Irish Gaelic in school.

This is how you say *hello* in Gaelic:

Dia dhuit (DEE-ah DWIT)

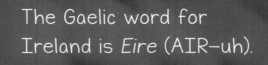
The Gaelic word for Ireland is *Eire* (AIR–uh).

SRÁID CHILL DARA
KILDARE STREET
2

a sign written in Irish Gaelic and English

21

Irish people have many types of jobs.

Some work on farms.

Irish dairy products are sold all over the world.

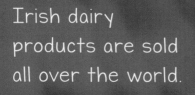

454g℮

KERRYGOLD
IRISH CREAMERY BUTTER

454g℮

KERRYGOLD™

IRISH CREAMERY BUTTER

Other people work in **tourism**.

They guide visitors through places like Blarney Castle.

People in Ireland make lots of yummy foods.

One is Irish soda bread.

This sweet bread can be made with currants or raisins.

Colcannon is a mixture of mashed potatoes and cabbage.

Many Irish people eat a hearty breakfast that includes eggs, rashers, and sausage. *Rashers* is another name for bacon or ham.

Several **breeds** of dogs were first raised in Ireland.

Irish terrier

Irish setter

One of the tallest breeds is the Irish wolfhound.

It can grow up to 2 feet 8 inches (81 cm) at the shoulder!

Irish wolfhounds were once used to hunt wolves.

Horse racing is a very popular sport in Ireland.

The Laytown Strand Races are held on a beach.

Hurling is an Irish field sport. It's played with a stick called a hurley.

Fast Facts

Capital city: Dublin

Population of Ireland: Almost five million people

Main languages: English and Irish Gaelic

Money: Euro

Major religion: Catholic

Neighboring country: Northern Ireland (UK)

Cool Fact: Traditional Irish step dancers perform all over the world. The dancers jump and move their feet very quickly while holding their arms straight.

breeds (BREEDZ) groups of animals with similar characteristics

capital (KAP-uh-tuhl) a city where a country's government is based

famine (FAM-in) a shortage of food

tourism (TOOR-iz-uhm) the business of providing information, transportation, and other services to travelers

uprising (UP-*rye*-zing) a revolt or riot

Index

Read More

Harvey, Miles. *Look What Came from Ireland.* New York: Franklin Watts (2002).

Koponen, Libby. *Ireland (A True Book).* New York: Scholastic (2009).

Learn More Online

To learn more about Ireland, visit
www.bearportpublishing.com/CountriesWeComeFrom

About the Author

Janice Clark Rudolph is a writer whose grandmothers emigrated from Ireland to the United States. She enjoys singing, acting, and studying family history.